WINE

Anxiety

FROM CONFUSED
TO CONFIDENT

BY ALENE KEENAN, THE YACHT STEW GURU

This book is a work of nonfiction. While every effort has been made to ensure accuracy, the author and publisher assume no responsibility for errors or omissions. The advice and recommendations provided are based on personal experience and professional opinion.

Published by Alene Keenan
La Crosse, Wisconsin, USA
Cover and interior design by Nauman Akbar
Printed in the United States of America
ISBN (Paperback): 9798832999722
ASIN: B0B3RSVK5D ISBN
(eBook): ASIN: B0B36D6QWP
First edition published 2020
Updated edition published 2025
For more information,
visit: www.etiquetteuncorked.com

Table of Contents

Dedication

To those who have ever hesitated before ordering a glass, felt unsure while holding a wine list, or feared they'd pronounce a name wrong—this book is for you.

You are not alone. I've met countless people, from first- time servers to seasoned yacht professionals, who've told me how confusing and intimidating wine can feel. The unspoken rules, the pressure to know the "right" things—it can strip away the joy and make something simple feel out of reach.

But wine is meant to bring people together.

That's why I wrote Wine Anxiety: From Confused to Confident—to offer a kinder, simpler, more empowering approach to wine. This book was born out of years spent living and working on private yachts, where hospitality is a lifestyle, and confidence in service is everything. My goal is to share what I've learned in a way that makes sense— wherever you are in your wine journey.

Thank you to every crew member, student, and guest who helped shape my story. This is for you.

With gratitude and cheers,

Alene Keenan

Preface to the New Edition

Wine has its own language, and for many people, it's hard to know where to begin.

When I started teaching wine courses for yacht crew, I realized how often people felt overwhelmed—not because they lacked interest, but because the information was scattered, the rules unclear, and the culture unwelcoming. Wine Anxiety: From Confused to Confident was created as a practical, approachable guide for anyone who wants to understand wine—without the pressure, jargon, or fear of "getting it wrong."

This new edition weaves in more of what I learned at sea, where service isn't just a task—it's an art form. From elegant dinners on deck to casual glasses shared among crew, wine has always been part of the connection.

Whether you're brushing up on your wine vocabulary, learning to taste like a pro, or just hoping to enjoy a glass without second-guessing yourself—I hope this book helps you feel informed, empowered, and maybe even a little inspired.

Let's make wine approachable—and fun. Warmly,

Alene

Introduction

For decades, I lived and worked at sea— providing service to elite clientele from across the globe on board some of the world's most exclusive private yachts. As a Chief Stewardess, I was responsible for creating seamless luxury experiences where nothing short of perfection was acceptable. Every detail mattered—from the way a napkin was folded to the wine poured into a glass. Over time, I became known for my expertise in hospitality and service, eventually earning the nickname "The Yacht Guru."

After years of circling the globe and writing a monthly column for The Triton, a leading trade publication for yacht professionals, I published The Yacht Guru's Bible, a comprehensive training manual for yacht stews. That led to a decade of teaching internationally accredited courses in topics like Silver Service, Wine and Cocktails, and Yacht Interior Management.

Among all the classes I taught, the wine course stood out. Students often told me they learned more in that half-day session than in years of wine tastings or trial-and-error. Why? Because I didn't teach wine as a sommelier—I taught it the way stews needed to understand it: clearly, practically, and with a dash of elegance.

That course became the heart of this book. Now that I've returned to my hometown here in the Midwest my mission is to bring the same level of confidence and hospitality I cultivated at sea to people here on land.

Whether you're ordering wine at a restaurant, selecting a bottle for a client dinner, or simply wanting to enjoy wine without second-guessing yourself, this book was created for you.

Wine Anxiety: From Confused to Confident is a down-to-earth guide to help you understand wine fundamentals, navigate wine lists with ease, and speak the language of wine—without feeling intimidated. We'll explore how wine is made, why grape varieties matter, how to decode wine labels, and how to taste like a pro. Most of all, I'll show you that wine doesn't have to be overwhelming. It can be joyful, empowering, and even a bit magical.

Let's raise a glass to learning, confidence, and never feeling lost in the wine aisle again.

— Alene Keenan

Founder, Etiquette Uncorked

Author, The Yacht Guru's Bible & Wine Anxiety: From Confused to Confident

Acknowledgments

This book is a tribute to the many people who have shaped my journey—both at sea and ashore—and to the incredible community that continues to support and inspire high standards in service.

To the captains and crew I've worked with over the years— thank you. Your high expectations, teamwork, and professionalism helped shape my understanding of what great service truly means. I've been lucky to work alongside exceptional people and learn from each experience.

To The Triton newspaper—thank you for publishing my articles for so many years and for giving yacht crew a voice in the industry. A special thank-you to founding editors Lucy Chabot Reed and David Reed for your vision, leadership, and encouragement. Writing for The Triton was more than a byline— it gave me the confidence and inspiration to create my first book, The Yacht Guru's Bible, and helped shape the path I'm still on today.

To the crew agencies and management companies who trusted me to train their teams—your support gave me the opportunity to share what I've learned and to help others grow.

To Maritime Professional Training in Fort Lauderdale— thank you for giving me a platform to teach and grow. Your early commitment to professional education helped raise the bar for the global yachting industry. MPT was one of the first U.S. schools to offer training at this level, and I'm proud to have been part of that effort.

A heartfelt thank-you to Lisa Morley, whose leadership and support made it all possible, and to the late, beloved Amy Beavers, whose internationally recognized expertise and passion for maritime education left an indelible mark on the industry and in our hearts.

To the Professional Yachting Association, and especially Joey Meen—thank you for your leadership and commitment to professional development in our industry. I'm proud to have contributed to the creation of the GUEST Program (Guidelines for Unified Excellence in Service Training). Helping establish global service standards and creating a clear training path for interior crew has been one of the most meaningful parts of my career.

To my friends, family, and business community here in the Midwest—thank you for your support and encouragement. You've given me the grounding and confidence I needed to bring this work home.

To the hospitality teams, wine professionals, and curious learners I've met along the way—thank you for sharing your enthusiasm and keeping the conversation going. Your passion and questions inspire me to keep learning and sharing.

And to anyone who's ever felt unsure around wine—this book is for you. I hope it gives you confidence, clarity, and enjoyment.

With appreciation,

Alene Keenan

INTRODUCTION TO WINE

Like many service professionals, my journey into the world of wine began in a restaurant. At the time, I assumed Chardonnay was just a fancy word for white wine and thought all red wine was called Burgundy simply because of its deep color. My limited understanding quickly became apparent when I transitioned to working on private yachts, where wine knowledge was not just a skill—it was an expectation.

Suddenly, I was responsible for curating wine lists, managing inventory, and confidently discussing selections with high-profile guests who knew far more about wine than I did. The labels were confusing, the terminology was overwhelming, and I had no idea where to start.

Over time, through study, tastings, and hands-on experience, I deciphered the language of wine and developed a practical, approachable way to understand it. I realized that wine isn't about memorizing obscure facts—it's about experiencing it. This book is designed to do the same for you.

Whether you're a service professional, a wine enthusiast, or simply someone who enjoys a glass of wine but wants to feel more confident, we'll break down the basics into clear, digestible sections.

Let's begin with the fundamentals of what wine is and how it's classified.

WHAT IS WINE? UNDERSTANDING THE FOUR "V's"

At its core, wine is an alcoholic beverage made from fermented grape juice. While wine can be made from other fruits, such as apples or plums, those must be labeled accordingly (e.g., "apple wine").

When selecting a wine, there are four key factors that influence its taste, quality, and style. These factors—often found on a wine label—are the Vineyard, Varietal, Vintner, and Vintage.

1. VINEYARD: ·Where It All Begins

A vineyard is where wine begins—it's the place where grapes are grown, and its location plays a vital role in shaping a wine's flavor profile. Climate, soil composition, and farming practices all influence the quality and characteristics of the grapes. This concept is known as terroir—the idea that the land itself imparts a unique fingerprint on the wine, capturing the essence of place in every bottle.

The study of grape cultivation is called viticulture, and specialists known as viticulturists work closely with winemakers (vintners) to ensure the highest grape quality for winemaking.

Some of the world's most prestigious vineyards are found in France (Bordeaux, Burgundy), Italy (Tuscany, Piedmont), and the United States (Napa Valley, Oregon's Willamette Valley).

2. VARIETAL VS. VARIETY: ·What's the Difference?

The term variety refers to the grape itself (e.g., Chardonnay, Merlot, Pinot Noir).

A varietal wine is one made primarily from a single grape variety—usually at least 75%-85% of one type, depending on the country's labeling laws.

For example, a bottle labeled Chardonnay is a varietal wine made mostly from Chardonnay grapes. A wine labeled Red Blend combines multiple grape varieties.

3. VINTNER: ·The Art of Winemaking

A vintner is a winemaker—someone responsible for the production of wine. Some vintners work at small, family-run wineries, while others oversee large-scale wine operations producing thousands of bottles annually.

Beyond their technical skill, experienced or well-known vintners often bring a signature style and reputation that can elevate the prestige of a wine brand, making their name as influential as the vineyard itself.

Did You Know?

- Many celebrities have invested in wineries, including actors, musicians, and athletes.

- There are over 65,000 wine producers worldwide, with approximately 14,000 in the United States.

- Globally, there are between 100,000 and 200,000 different wine brands.

4. VINTAGE: Why the Year Matters

The vintage refers to the year the grapes were harvested. Since grape quality depends heavily on weather conditions, some years produce better vintages than others.

A great vintage means the weather was optimal for grape-growing, resulting in a higher-quality wine. A poor vintage might mean unexpected weather challenges affected the grapes' development.

In recent years, global warming has added new unpredictability to growing seasons—shifting harvest times, increasing the risk of drought or extreme heat, and forcing many winemakers to adapt their practices to preserve the integrity of their wines.

A BRIEF HISTORY OF WINE

Wine has been part of human history for over 8,000 years, dating back to 6000 BC. However, the American wine industry is relatively young in comparison.

The first commercial U.S. winery was established in the early 1800s.

Prohibition (1920–1933) nearly wiped out winemaking in the United States.

It wasn't until the 1960s and 1970s that the U.S. wine industry began its remarkable comeback, leading to the global recognition of California wines. Today, American wines, especially from Napa Valley and Sonoma, are considered some of the best in the world.

OVERCOMING WINE ANXIETY

For many, learning about wine can feel intimidating. I've seen this firsthand during my time on private yachts, fine dining events, and curated wine experiences where guests often hesitated to ask questions, fearing they would sound uninformed.

The reality? Wine is meant to be enjoyed—not feared.

A huge part of building wine confidence is being open to new experiences and trusting your own palate. There are no wrong preferences—just personal taste.

One of the most important lessons I've learned is that wine is not about snobbery—it's about pleasure and connection. Whether you're choosing wine for a dinner party, a romantic evening, or simply unwinding at the end of the day, the best wine is the one you enjoy.

WHITE, RED, AND ROSÉ WINES: UNDERSTANDING THE BASICS

All wines originate from grapes, which are either white (green/pink skins) or red (dark purple/blue skins). The core differences between white, red, and rosé wines come down to the grapes used and the production methods chosen.

- White wines are made by removing the skins and seeds before fermentation, resulting in a lighter, crisper style.

- Red wines are fermented with the skins and seeds, which impart color, tannins, and bold flavors.

- Rosé wines are made from red grapes but with shorter skin contact, giving them a pink hue and a balance of red- wine fruitiness with white-wine freshness.

Another key factor in wine production is fermentation—the process where yeast converts grape sugars into alcohol. The choice of fermentation vessel (oak barrels vs. stainless steel tanks) also impacts a wine's final character.

- Oak barrels add flavor nuances like vanilla, spice, and caramel, softening the wine's tannins.

- Stainless steel tanks preserve freshness and purity, allowing the grape's natural character to shine.

WINE AND CHEMISTRY:
THE ART BEHIND THE GLASS

At its core, wine is a balance of science and art. Water and ethanol (alcohol) make up 98% of wine.

The remaining 2% consists of acids, sugars, esters, glycerin, pigments, and tannins—all of which influence aroma, flavor, and texture.

This complex interaction is why every bottle of wine is unique, even from the same vineyard or winemaker.

FINAL THOUGHTS:
YOUR JOURNEY INTO WINE STARTS HERE

Now that you understand the fundamentals of wine, you're ready to build confidence in your selections and enjoy wine without intimidation.

The world of wine is vast, but remember:

- Trust your own taste.

- Be open to new experiences.

Understanding these core wine concepts benefits everyone— from executives and hospitality professionals to casual wine enthusiasts. For leaders, confidently choosing and discussing wine enhances presence in business and social settings. For hospitality staff, wine knowledge elevates guest experiences and reflects professionalism. Enthusiasts will find that a stronger foundation improves enjoyment, removes intimidation, and sharpens selection skills. As we go forward, we'll build on this knowledge to help you feel confident in any wine-related setting. Enjoy the journey!

THREE CHALLENGES THAT CREATE WINE ANXIETY

For many people, choosing and buying wine can be intimidating. Whether it's deciphering a label, navigating a wine list at a restaurant, or selecting a bottle in a wine shop, the experience can feel like being in a foreign country without knowing the language.

This uncertainty isn't unique to wine enthusiasts. Even hospitality professionals and yacht crew—who are expected to serve wine confidently—often struggle at first. When I began working on private yachts, I was responsible for maintaining wine inventories and assisting high-profile guests with their selections. At first, I was overwhelmed by the labels, unfamiliar terminology, and expectations of knowledge.

Through experience, I learned that wine anxiety is not about a lack of intelligence—it's about a lack of familiarity.

The good news? Once you understand a few key principles, the fear disappears, and confidence takes its place.

Let's break it down into three major challenges that create wine anxiety—and how to overcome them.

CHALLENGE #1:
Navigating the Wine Shop

The Overwhelming Selection

Walking into a wine shop or supermarket can be overwhelming. Thousands of bottles line the shelves, varying in brand, region, grape variety, style, and price. Wines can be single-varietal or blends, categorized by color, country, or style (sparkling, dessert, or fortified). With so many choices, it's no wonder many people feel lost.

Fear of Making the Wrong Choice

Many shoppers hesitate for fear of choosing the "wrong" bottle, overspending, or appearing unsophisticated. The solution? Ask for help. Wine shop employees are there to guide you.

Here's how to simplify your wine shopping experience:

- Know your preference. Do you enjoy dry or sweet wines? Light or full-bodied?

- Consider the occasion. Is this for a casual evening or a special dinner?

- Think about food pairings. Let the staff know what you'll be eating.

- Set a budget. Good wines exist at every price point.

When I worked on yachts, I had access to incredible wines from around the world, yet I still had to ask suppliers and sommeliers for guidance. Over time, I built my knowledge— and you will too.

CHALLENGE #2:
Ordering Wine at a Restaurant

The Pressure of the Wine List

Dining out is a social experience, and every host wants their dining partners to enjoy the wine selection. Uncertainty about selecting the right wine can feel high-stakes— especially when dining with colleagues, clients, or friends. The fear of ordering a disappointing bottle, mispronouncing a name, or choosing something that doesn't pair well with the food can make the experience stressful.

In fine dining and yachting, wine service is an integral part of hospitality. Professional chefs pay close attention to pairing wine with their food. When I was onboard, I had to confidently present and serve wine to CEOs, celebrities, and royalty. I learned that the key to success isn't memorizing every wine—it's knowing how to ask the right questions and describe preferences.

How to Order Wine with Confidence:

- Decide on your meal first. Matching wine to your food makes the choice easier.

- Use basic descriptive words. Instead of worrying about wine jargon, tell the staff what you like: "I prefer crisp, citrusy whites" or "I like bold reds with a smooth finish."

- Don't be afraid to ask for help. Helping customers with their choices is an extension of the staff's hospitality. Sommeliers and servers are there to assist, and a good one won't pressure you into the most expensive bottle. A reputable establishment wants to make you happy with wine in every price range.

- Set a price range subtly. If you don't want to say your budget out loud, point to a wine on the list and say, "I'm looking for something in this range."

The Price Factor

Many people assume expensive wines are always better. While price can indicate quality, it's not a guarantee. A good restaurant or yacht wine cellar will offer excellent wines at all price points. Your goal isn't to impress—it's to find a wine you enjoy.

CHALLENGE #3:
Decoding Wine Labels

Understanding wine labels is one of the biggest hurdles for wine buyers. Unlike food packaging, wine labels vary greatly between countries and styles.

The world of wine is divided into two categories:

Old World Wines (Europe, North Africa, Middle East)

- Labels focus on the region (e.g., Bordeaux, Burgundy, Chianti).

- The grape variety is not always listed, so you need to know which grapes grow in those areas.

- Strict regulations define how wines must be made.

New World Wines (United States, South America, Australia, South Africa)

- Labels prominently display the grape variety (e.g., Chardonnay, Merlot, Cabernet Sauvignon).

- Branding and marketing play a bigger role. Typically easier to understand for beginners.

How Yacht Stewards & Hospitality Professionals Benefit from Label Knowledge

Working on yachts gave me an advantage—I encountered both Old World and New World wines while provisioning in different countries. Spending time in French, Italian, and Spanish ports meant I had to learn quickly. But even on land, you can develop the same skill.

When selecting a bottle, focus on four key pieces of information:

- Grape variety & region (especially important for Old World wines).

- Winery or producer (well-known wineries often indicate quality).

- Vintage year (some years are better than others for certain wines).

- Alcohol by Volume (ABV) (higher alcohol often means riper, fuller-bodied wine).

Over time, recognizing labels and understanding regions becomes second nature—just like it did for me on yachts. Check out Appendix II in the back of the book.

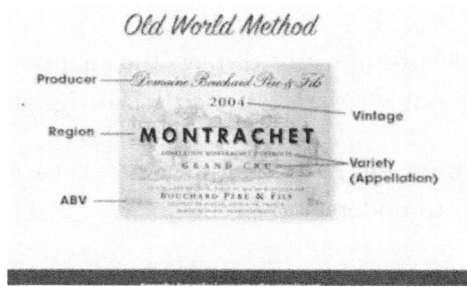

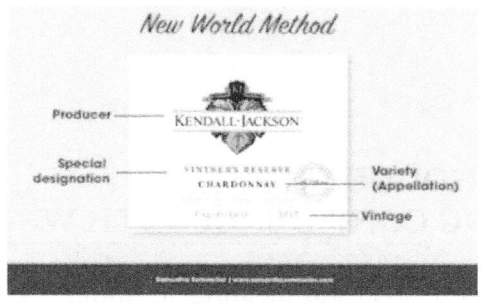

Insider Tip: How Marketing Influences Wine Buying:

- Wine is emotional. Marketers know this, which is why labels use carefully chosen words and imagery to influence your perception.

- Descriptive sensory terms (e.g., "lush, silky, vibrant") create an image before you even taste the wine.

- Branding matters. Some people gravitate toward familiar labels, while others prefer boutique wineries

- Price psychology. A higher price doesn't always mean better quality—but it can influence how people perceive a wine's value.

When working with high-end clients on yachts, I saw firsthand how wine branding and price influenced choices. Some guests would choose a wine just for the name or prestige, while others would seek unique, small-production wines.

The takeaway? Trust your own taste—not just the marketing.

FINAL THOUGHTS:
BUILDING CONFIDENCE WITH WINE

Wine shouldn't feel intimidating. It should be enjoyable, social, and rewarding. By breaking down the challenges of buying wine, ordering at restaurants, and understanding labels, you'll feel more confident in any wine-related situation.

Remember:

- *Ask for help—wine professionals exist to guide you.*

- *Know what you like—flavor descriptions matter more than fancy terms.*

- *Practice makes perfect—the more you explore, the more confident you'll become.*

Understanding how to confidently select, order, and discuss wine is vital for executive presence, hospitality professionals, and wine enthusiasts alike.

For executives, the ability to navigate a wine list, make thoughtful selections, and engage in wine-related conversations enhances credibility and confidence in professional dining and networking settings.

Hospitality workers, including restaurant staff and yacht stews, benefit from knowledgeable wine service, menu pairings, and label recognition, which elevate guest experiences and demonstrate expertise.

Wine enthusiasts gain the ability to shop, order, and explore wines without intimidation, making every experience more enjoyable.

As we move forward, we will build on this foundation, diving deeper into wine-tasting techniques, pairing strategies, and practical applications to further develop confidence and ease in any wine-related setting. Before long, you'll feel just as comfortable talking about wine as you do enjoying it!

THE IMPORTANCE
OF GRAPES

Wine knowledge can seem endless, but no one is expected to master every subtlety. Instead, focusing on the grapes themselves provides a strong foundation for understanding wine. Every grape variety has unique characteristics, influencing the flavors, aromas, and textures of the wine it produces.

When I worked on private yachts, I was constantly exposed to high-end wine lists and rare vintages from around the world. At first, it was overwhelming. But once I learned how grape varieties shaped a wine's style, I was able to confidently recommend wines, pair them with meals, and create memorable experiences for guests.

In this chapter, we'll explore the Noble Grapes, the most widely recognized varieties that grow across the world's major wine regions.

Understanding these grapes will help you recognize flavors, choose wines with confidence, and develop a deeper appreciation for what's in your glass.

WHAT ARE THE NOBLE GRAPES?

Noble Grapes—also known as International Varieties—are grape types that are widely grown and consistently produce high-quality wines across different regions.

Some say there are six Noble Grapes, while others expand the list to 18 or even 75. Check out Appendix I for a list of the 18 Noble Grapes.

Three White Noble Grapes:

- Riesling

- Sauvignon Blanc

- Chardonnay

Three Red Noble Grapes:

- Pinot Noir

- Merlot

- Cabernet Sauvignon

Learning these six varieties will help you recognize patterns in flavor, acidity, and structure, making it easier to navigate wine lists, shop for wine, and pair wines with food.

FLAVOR PROFILES OF THE THREE WHITE NOBLE GRAPES

When thinking about white wine flavors, imagine walking through the produce section of a grocery store. White wines generally fall into categories of citrus fruits, orchard fruits, stone fruits, and tropical fruits.

1. **Riesling**

   - *Body: Light*

   - *Acidity: High*

   - *Flavor Profile: Citrus (lime, lemon), orchard or tree fruits (apple, pear), stone fruit (peach, nectarine), floral notes, and minerality.*

- Origin: Germany and Alsace (France)

- *Style: Ranges from bone-dry to sweet.*

Why It Matters: Riesling is one of the most versatile wines and pairs exceptionally well with spicy food, seafood, and even certain cheeses. On yachts, Riesling was often served with Asian-fusion cuisine or light appetizers.

2. **Sauvignon Blanc**

   - Body: Medium

   - Acidity: High

   - Flavor Profile: Citrus (grapefruit, lime), tropical fruit (passionfruit), and herbal / green notes (grass, bell pepper).

   - Origin: Bordeaux and Loire Valley (France)

   - Style: Crisp, dry, and refreshing.

Why It Matters: Sauvignon Blanc is a go-to white wine for warm-weather sipping and pairs well with salads, seafood, and goat cheese. It was frequently served during sunset aperitifs on the aft deck of yachts.

3. **Chardonnay**

   - Body: Medium to full Acidity: Balanced

   - Flavor Profile: Citrus, orchard fruit (apple, pear), tropical fruit (pineapple, mango), with vanilla, butter, and spice when aged in oak.

- Origin: Burgundy (France)

- Style: Can be crisp and unoaked or rich and buttery depending on production methods.

Why It Matters: Chardonnay is one of the most adaptable wines—it can be fresh and mineral-driven or creamy and luxurious. On private yachts, Chablis (unoaked Chardonnay from France) was often requested with oysters, while rich, oaked Chardonnays were popular with lobster dishes.

FLAVOR PROFILES OF THE THREE RED NOBLE GRAPES

For red wines, think about berries and dark fruits. Red wines fall into a flavor spectrum from red berries (strawberry, raspberry) to dark cherries, plums, blackberries, and even dried fruits.

1. Pinot Noir

- Body: Light to medium Acidity: Medium to high

- Flavor Profile: Red fruit (cherry, raspberry), earthy (mushroom, forest floor), and vanilla / spice from oak aging.

- Origin: Burgundy (France)

- Style: Elegant, complex, and food-friendly.

Why It Matters: Pinot Noir is a favorite among fine dining guests because of its delicate flavors and ability to pair with a wide range of dishes. On yachts, Pinot Noir was often chosen for intimate dinners where guests wanted something elegant but not overpowering.

2. Merlot

- Body: Medium Acidity: Medium

- Flavor Profile: Dark fruit (plum, black cherry), herbal / spice notes, and soft tannins.

- Origin: Bordeaux (France)

- Style: Smooth and easy-drinking.

Why It Matters: Merlot is often the "introductory" red wine because of its soft, fruit-driven style. On yachts, it was frequently requested by guests who wanted a red wine that wasn't too heavy or tannic.

3. Cabernet Sauvignon

- Body: Full

- Acidity: Medium to high

- Flavor Profile: Dark fruit (blackcurrant, blackberry), spice (black pepper, tobacco), and vanilla from oak aging.

- Origin: Bordeaux (France)

- Style: Bold, structured, and age-worthy.

Why It Matters: Cabernet Sauvignon is the most recognized red grape in the world. Its bold structure makes it the perfect pairing for steaks and rich dishes—a favorite on yachts for formal dining nights.

THE SCIENCE OF WINE AROMAS: Why Does Wine Smell Like Fruit, Herbs, or Spices?

Winemaking is a chemical process, and the aromas we associate with wine come from compounds naturally found in other foods and plants:

Terpenes = *Floral, citrus, and herbal aromas (also found in pine and lavender).*

Pyrazines = *Green bell pepper and grassy notes (common in Sauvignon Blanc).*

Esters = *Fruity aromas (citrus, apple, banana).*

Lactones = *Nutty, toasted, or coconut aromas (from oak aging).*

Malolactic Fermentation = *Buttery, creamy texture (common in oaked Chardonnay).*

On yachts, I had to quickly learn how to describe wines to guests who had specific preferences. Understanding these aroma compounds made it easier to guide wine choices based on the flavors guests enjoyed in food.

FINAL THOUGHTS:
WHY GRAPE KNOWLEDGE MATTERS

Learning the characteristics of these six Noble Grapes is the first step to becoming comfortable with wine. Whether you're a wine enthusiast, hospitality professional, or executive looking to refine your presence, knowing these grapes will:

- Help you identify wines you enjoy.

- Make it easier to shop, order, and pair wines confidently.

- Give you a framework for understanding wine lists and labels.

As we continue, we will build on this foundation—exploring wine-tasting techniques, food pairings, and how to expand your wine knowledge beyond the basics. With time, choosing and enjoying wine will feel effortless!

IMPORTANT WINE
GROWING REGIONS

Wine is profoundly shaped by its place of origin. Climate, soil, and regional traditions—together known as terroir— influence a wine's flavor, structure, and aging potential. Gaining familiarity with key wine regions not only helps you navigate wine lists with confidence but also deepens your appreciation for the diversity and character found in every bottle.

When I worked on private yachts, I had the opportunity to taste wines from all over the world. Many guests onboard were serious wine collectors, and I needed to understand both classic Old World wines and bold, innovative New World wines. I quickly learned that the same grape variety could taste vastly different depending on where it was grown and how it was produced.

By learning the major wine regions, you can start to recognize why wines taste the way they do—and even predict what you might enjoy before ever opening the bottle.

NEW WORLD VS. OLD WORLD WINE REGIONS:

What's the Difference?

The world of wine is divided into two major categories:

Old World Wines (Traditional, Terroir-Driven)

- *Countries: France, Italy, Spain, Germany, Portugal, Austria, Greece, and others.*

- *History: Wine has been made here for thousands of years.*

- *Style: Wines tend to be lighter, earthier, more acidic, and lower in alcohol than New World wines.*

- *Labeling: Labels focus on region (appellation) rather than grape variety. You have to know which grapes are grown in each region.*

- *Production: Winemaking is governed by strict rules and regulations to maintain tradition.*

New World Wines (Bold, Fruit-Forward, Innovative)

- *Countries: United States, Australia, New Zealand, South Africa, Argentina, Chile, and others.*

- *History: Winemaking is relatively young, typically less than 400 years old.*

- *Style: Wines are often fuller-bodied, fruitier, and higher in alcohol due to warmer climates.*

- *Labeling: Labels typically list the grape variety, making it easier for consumers to understand.*

- *Production: Fewer restrictions allow for innovation and experimentation in winemaking techniques.*

How This Knowledge Helped Me on Yachts

On yachts, we catered to guests with a range of wine preferences. Some requested iconic Bordeaux or Burgundy wines with dinner, while others loved the bold fruit flavors of Napa Cabernet Sauvignon or Australian

Shiraz. Understanding Old World vs. New World styles made it easier to recommend wines and explain the differences without overwhelming them with jargon.

FAMOUS FRENCH WINE REGIONS YOU SHOULD KNOW

French wines are a benchmark for quality and influence winemaking worldwide. France is home to all six Noble Grapes, and its terroir-driven approach has shaped global wine culture.

There are 17 wine regions in France, but let's focus on four of the most important: Check out Appendix III for maps.

1. **Alsace (Riesling & Aromatic Whites)**

   - *Location: Northeast France, bordering Germany.*

   - *Famous For: Riesling, Gewürztraminer, Pinot Gris.*

   - *Climate: Cool, producing crisp, floral, and mineral-driven wines.*

   - *Style: Dry to sweet aromatic whites with high acidity and strong food-pairing potential.*

Why It Matters: If you enjoy German-style wines, you'll love Alsace Riesling. On yachts, Riesling was often served with spicy Asian dishes or seafood platters.

2. **Burgundy (Pinot Noir & Chardonnay)**

    - *Location:* *Central France, southeast of Paris.*

    - *Famous For:* *Pinot Noir (red), Chardonnay (white).*

    - *Climate:* *Cool to moderate, producing elegant, high-acid wines.*

    - *Style:* *Light-bodied Pinot Noir with red fruit and earthy notes; mineral-driven Chardonnay (especially in Chablis).*

    - *Fact:* *Burgundy wines are almost never blended—they reflect the land.*

Why It Matters: Burgundy sets the global standard for Pinot Noir and Chardonnay. Many guests on yachts requested Premier Cru and Grand Cru Burgundies, known for their delicate complexity.

1. **Loire Valley (Sauvignon Blanc & Chenin Blanc)**

    - *Location:* *Northwest France, following the Loire River.*

    - *Famous For:* *Sauvignon Blanc (Sancerre, Pouilly-Fumé), Chenin Blanc (Vouvray).*

    - *Climate:* *Cool, producing fresh, zesty whites and light-bodied reds.*

    - *Style:* *High-acid, aromatic whites with floral, citrus, and mineral notes.*

Why It Matters: If you love crisp, refreshing wines, Loire Valley Sauvignon Blanc is a great choice. On yachts, Sancerre was a staple with oysters, shellfish, and goat cheese.

2. **Bordeaux (Cabernet Sauvignon & Merlot Blends)**

   - *Location:* Southwest France, near the Atlantic Ocean.

   - *Famous For:* Cabernet Sauvignon, Merlot, Sauvignon Blanc.

   - *Climate:* Moderate, with variations between Left Bank (Cabernet-driven) and Right Bank (Merlot-driven).

   - *Style:* Bold reds with dark fruit, tannins, and oak aging.

   - *Fact:* Bordeaux is the largest fine wine region in the world, with over 50 appellations.

Why It Matters: Bordeaux produces some of the most prestigious wines in history, including Château Margaux, Château Latour, and Château Lafite Rothschild. On yachts, these were frequently requested for special occasions.

French Wine Growing Regions

NEW WORLD WINE REGIONS TO KNOW

While Old World regions focus on tradition and terroir, New World regions prioritize innovation and expression. Here are four of the most influential:

1. **Napa Valley, USA (Cabernet Sauvignon)**

    -   ***Best Known For:*** *Rich, powerful Cabernet Sauvignon with black fruit, spice, and vanilla notes.*

- **Why It's Important:** *Napa Cabs rival Bordeaux in quality and price.*

- **On Yachts:** *Often requested by American guests who preferred bold reds.*

2. **Mendoza, Argentina (Malbec)**

   - **Best Known For:** *Smooth, fruit-forward Malbec with blackberry, plum, and cocoa notes.*

   - **Why It's Important:** *Argentina revived Malbec, making it globally popular.*

   - **On Yachts:** *Served with grilled meats or tapas-style dinners.*

3. **Marlborough, New Zealand (Sauvignon Blanc)**

   - **Best Known For:** *Crisp, citrusy Sauvignon Blanc with passionfruit and herbaceous notes.*

   - **Why It's Important:** *One of the world's most recognized white wines.*

   - **On Yachts:** *A favorite for daytime lounging and seafood pairings.*

4. **Barossa Valley, Australia (Shiraz)**

   - **Best Known For:** *Bold, spicy Shiraz with dark berry, chocolate, and pepper notes.*

   - **Why It's Important:** *Australian Shiraz is powerful yet smooth, loved by red wine drinkers.*

- ***On Yachts:*** *Often paired with grilled lamb or barbecue.*

FINAL THOUGHTS: WHY WINE REGIONS MATTER

Knowing where a wine comes from helps you predict its flavors, structure, and quality. Whether you're:

- Hosting a dinner party

- Ordering wine at a restaurant

- Stocking a yacht's wine cellar

This knowledge builds confidence and makes choosing wine more enjoyable.

Understanding key wine regions is essential for executive presence, hospitality professionals, and wine enthusiasts because it provides a strong foundation for confidently selecting, discussing, and appreciating wine. For executives, knowledge of Old World vs. New World wines enhances their ability to navigate business dinners and networking events with ease.

Hospitality workers, especially restaurant staff and yacht stewards, benefit from recognizing regional wine styles, pairing recommendations, and guest preferences, elevating the level of service they provide.

For wine enthusiasts, knowing where a wine comes from helps predict its flavors, structure, and quality, making wine shopping and ordering more enjoyable. As we move forward, we will build on this foundation by exploring wine tasting techniques, food pairings, and advanced selection strategies to further develop confidence in any wine-related setting.

FUNDAMENTAL
CHARACTERISTICS OF WINE

Now that we've explored grape varieties and wine regions, it's time to break down the core characteristics that define every wine. Understanding these fundamental traits will help you describe what you like (or dislike) in a wine, navigate wine lists with confidence, and enhance your tasting experience.

On private yachts, I often served guests who knew what they enjoyed but struggled to articulate why they liked certain wines. Learning the five key characteristics of wine

—Sweetness, Acidity, Tannins, Alcohol, and Body—
allowed me to guide guests toward selections that suited
their preferences.

No matter what type of wine you drink, these characteristics
are always present. When properly balanced, they create a
harmonious wine. When one is too dominant, it can throw
the wine off-balance. Let's dive into what each of these
means and how they shape the wine in your glass.

THE FIVE FUNDAMENTAL CHARACTERISTICS OF WINE

WINE CHARACTERISTICS

Sweetness
Acidity
Tannin
Alcohol
Body

1. SWEETNESS: HOW SWEET OR DRY IS THE WINE?

Sweetness in wine comes from residual sugar left after
fermentation. Some wines are intentionally sweet, while

others are fermented until nearly all the sugar is gone, creating a dry wine.

Understanding Sweetness in Wine:

- Sweet wines have noticeable residual sugar and often appeal to new wine drinkers.

- Off-dry wines have a hint of sweetness but are not fully sweet.

- Dry wines have little to no residual sugar, even if they have fruity aromas that give the illusion of sweetness.

- ABV (Alcohol by Volume) as a Sweetness Guide:
    - Below 10% ABV → Often off-dry or sweet
    - 11–12.5% ABV → Typically off-dry

    - 12.5% ABV and above → Usually dry

Yacht Insight: Many first-time wine drinkers prefer sweeter wines, such as Riesling or Moscato, because the sweetness balances acidity. However, for guests looking for drier, complex wines, I guided them toward Chardonnay, Sauvignon Blanc, or dry Bordeaux blends.

2. ACIDITY:
THE LIVELINESS AND BRIGHTNESS OF WINE

Acidity is what gives wine its crispness and freshness. It creates a mouthwatering sensation and is essential for balance.

How Acidity Affects Wine:

- High-acid wines taste crisp, tart, and refreshing. Example: Sauvignon Blanc, Champagne.

- Low-acid wines feel rounder and softer on the palate. Example: Viognier, Merlot.

- Acidity is crucial for aging—high-acid wines tend to age better than low-acid wines.

Malolactic Fermentation & Creaminess:

- Some wines, especially Chardonnay, go through malolactic fermentation, which softens acidity and creates a creamy, buttery texture (due to the presence of diacetyl, the same compound found in butter-flavored popcorn).

- Most red wines naturally undergo malolactic fermentation, making their acidity feel less sharp.

Yacht Insight: Guests who wanted refreshing, zesty wines were often directed toward Loire Valley Sauvignon Blanc or crisp Chablis. Those who preferred richer, creamier whites enjoyed oaked California Chardonnay.

3. TANNINS:
THE STRUCTURE AND TEXTURE OF RED WINES

Tannins are naturally occurring polyphenol compounds found in grape skins, seeds, and stems. They create a drying, puckering sensation in the mouth and contribute to a wine's structure and aging potential.

Tannins in Wine:

- High tannin wines feel bold and drying (Cabernet Sauvignon, Nebbiolo).

- Low tannin wines feel softer and smoother (Pinot Noir, Gamay).

- Oak aging can add tannins, enhancing structure. Common Tannin Comparisons:

  o Think of over-steeped black tea—that drying, slightly bitter sensation is tannin.

  o Dark chocolate and coffee also contain tannins.

Yacht Insight: Some guests loved the power of tannic red wines, while others found them too intense. I often recommended softer reds like Merlot for beginners, while seasoned wine lovers enjoyed structured Bordeaux or Barolo.

4. ALCOHOL: THE WEIGHT AND WARMTH OF WINE

Alcohol contributes to a wine's body and texture. Wines with higher alcohol feel fuller and richer, while those with lower alcohol feel lighter and more delicate.

Alcohol & Body Connection:

- Low-alcohol wines (Under 12.5%) Light-bodied (Riesling, Pinot Grigio).

- Medium-alcohol wines (12.5–13.5%) → Medium-bodied (Sangiovese, Chardonnay).

- High-alcohol wines (14%+) → Full-bodied (Zinfandel, Syrah).

The Alcohol Burn:

- Too much alcohol can create a burning sensation in the throat.

- Balanced wines integrate alcohol seamlessly into the structure.

Yacht Insight: Onboard, some guests preferred lighter wines for daytime sipping, while others enjoyed full-bodied reds for formal dinners. Knowing the alcohol level helped me suggest wines appropriate for the occasion.

5. BODY:
THE WEIGHT AND TEXTURE OF WINE

Body describes how rich or heavy a wine feels in the mouth. It's influenced by alcohol, tannins, sugar, and winemaking techniques.

Comparing Wine Body to Milk:

- Light-bodied wines feel like skim milk (Pinot Grigio, Gamay).

- Medium-bodied wines feel like whole milk (Sangiovese, Grenache).

- Full-bodied wines feel like cream (Cabernet Sauvignon, Chardonnay aged in oak).

Yacht Insight: Guests often wanted light-bodied wines for daytime or seafood pairings and full-bodied wines for richer dishes like steak or truffle pasta.

Insider Tip: How To Use Back Labels To Understand Wine

Many wine bottles feature useful descriptions on the back label to help consumers understand their style.

What to Look for on the Back Label:
Descriptive Words:

- Style: Elegant, powerful, vibrant, complex.

- Texture: Silky, rich, smooth, bold.

- Winemaking Process:

    o Mentions of oak aging, malolactic fermentation, or terroir help indicate wine style.

Region & Grapes:

Some labels emphasize region (Bordeaux, Napa), while others highlight grape variety (Cabernet Sauvignon, Pinot Noir).

Yacht Insight: Many guests chose wines based on back label descriptions without realizing it. Learning how to interpret key wine terms helped me guide their selections more effectively.

FINAL THOUGHTS: MASTERING WINE CHARACTERISTICS

By understanding these five characteristics—Sweetness, Acidity, Tannins, Alcohol, and Body—you will be able to describe what you like, navigate wine selections with ease, and develop your tasting skills.

As we move forward, we'll build on this knowledge by exploring wine tasting techniques, food pairings, and advanced wine appreciation. Whether you're selecting a wine for a business dinner, fine dining service, or personal enjoyment, these fundamentals will give you the confidence to choose wisely and enjoy fully!

TASTE WINE LIKE A PRO

Now that you understand the essential characteristics of wine, it's time to explore the art of tasting.

Tasting wine is about more than just drinking—it's about engaging all your senses to fully appreciate the flavors, aromas, and textures in each glass. The way wine looks, smells, feels, and tastes provides valuable insight into its quality, structure, and style.

On private yachts, wine service was a key part of hospitality. I had to quickly learn how to taste and describe wines to help guests select the perfect bottle. Some guests were wine collectors with deep knowledge, while others simply wanted to enjoy a great glass without overcomplicating it.

The good news? Tasting wine like a pro isn't difficult. By following this simple four-step method—Sight, Swirl, Sniff, and Sip—you'll develop a refined palate and confidence in choosing wines you love.

THE FOUR-STEP SYSTEM FOR TASTING WINE

SIGHT	SWIRL	SNIFF	SIP

Look at the color and clarity.	Swirl your glass to release aromas.	Take a short sniff to enjoy aromas.	Sip the wine and savor the taste.

1. SIGHT: EXAMINING THE WINE

The first step in tasting wine is looking at it. The color and clarity of a wine reveal its age, grape variety, and even quality.

What to Look For:

Color Intensity:

- White wines range from pale greenish-yellow to deep gold.

- Rosé wines can be delicate peach to vibrant pink or purple.

- Red wines start as bright ruby or purple and turn brick or brown with age.

Clarity: A clear, bright wine is usually well-made. Cloudiness could indicate age, unfiltered winemaking, or a flaw.

Viscosity (Legs or Tears):

- Swirl the wine—if slow-moving legs form on the glass, it likely has higher alcohol or sugar (richer texture).

- Lighter wines have faster-moving, thinner legs.

Yacht Insight: Holding a wine up to natural light helped me assess its freshness and quality before serving guests. For aged wines, the color difference between the rim and the core provided clues about how well the wine had aged.

2. SWIRL: RELEASING AROMAS

Swirling wine introduces oxygen, which helps release its aromas. This step enhances your ability to smell and taste.

How to Swirl Like a Pro:

- Use a flat surface: Place your glass on a table and gently swirl the wine.

- Use the stem for control: Holding the stem prevents warming the wine.

- Avoid overfilling: A glass should be only one-third full to prevent spills.

Why It Matters:

- Swirling allows aromatic compounds to rise, making it easier to detect complex scents.

- Oxygen helps soften harsh tannins in young, bold red wines.

Yacht Insight: Swirling helped when serving fine wines that had been stored in the yacht's cellar—it brought out delicate aromas and softened tannins in structured reds.

3. SNIFF: IDENTIFYING AROMAS

Aromas play a huge role in how wine tastes—most of what we call "flavors" are actually detected through our sense of smell.

How to Sniff Wine Properly:

- Bring the glass to your nose and take a deep inhale.

- Note your first impression—fruit, flowers, spices?

- Swirl again and take a second, deeper sniff.

Understanding Wine Aromas:

- Primary Aromas (from grapes): Fruits, flowers, herbs.

- Secondary Aromas (from winemaking): Butter, toast, vanilla (from oak aging), yeast (from fermentation).

- Tertiary Aromas (from aging): Leather, tobacco, earthy, nutty, dried fruit.

Yacht Insight: Guests would often say, "I don't know what I'm smelling." I'd ask simple questions like:

"Do you smell citrus or berries?"

"Is there a hint of spice, vanilla, or chocolate?"

This guided their experience and helped them enjoy wine on a deeper level.

This guided their experience and helped them enjoy wine on a deeper level.

4. SIP: TASTING & ANALYZING WINE

Now, it's time to taste! Take a small sip and let the wine coat your mouth.

What to Focus On:

- Sweetness – Is the wine dry or slightly sweet?

- Acidity – Does it make your mouth water?

- Tannins (for reds) – Does it dry out your mouth?

- Alcohol – Do you feel warmth in your throat?

- Body & Texture – Is it light and crisp or rich and full- bodied?

Yacht Insight: Some guests enjoyed bold, full-bodied reds, while others preferred light, elegant wines. Tasting wine before serving it ensured I could describe it accurately and recommend the best food pairings.

Insider Tip: Tasting Takes Practice

Developing Your Wine Memory Takes Time.

The more you taste, the more you train your brain to recognize flavors and aromas.

Wine creates emotional and taste memories—over time, you'll recall specific wines and regions easily.

Common Wine Tasting Mistakes:

- Drinking too quickly instead of analyzing.

- Not using a white background to observe color.

- Judging a wine on one sip—let it evolve in the glass.

Yacht Insight: Some guests were eager to expand their wine knowledge but felt intimidated by "expert" descriptions. Breaking it down into simple comparisons (e.g., "This tastes like blackberry jam with a hint of spice") made the experience more approachable.

MASTERING WINE TASTING

Now that you know how to taste wine like a pro, you'll be able to:

- ✓ Recognize key aromas and flavors.

- ✓ Describe wines confidently in restaurants, shops, and social settings.

- ✓ Identify what you like and why—leading to better wine choices.

- ✓ Pair wine with food more effectively.

What You've Learned So Far:

- ☑ How to overcome wine anxiety.

- ☑ The six original Noble Grapes.

- ☑ The importance of wine-growing regions.

- ☑ How to read a wine label.

- ☑ The five fundamental characteristics of wine.

- ☑ The four-step method for tasting wine like a pro.

Why This Matters

- For Executives: Wine knowledge enhances professional presence in business and networking settings.

- For Hospitality Professionals: Being able to taste and describe wines accurately is crucial for service.

- For Wine Enthusiasts: Mastering the basics makes wine more enjoyable and approachable.

Whether you're studying wine for work or personal enjoyment, the goal is to feel more confident in your choices and to continue learning and expanding your palate.

FINAL THOUGHTS:
ENJOYING WINE WITH CONFIDENCE

Wine is one of life's greatest pleasures, yet for many, it feels intimidating. Whether you are learning about wine for work, social settings, or personal enjoyment, this book has provided essential tools to boost your confidence.

You now know how to:

- ✓ Understand wine characteristics.

- ✓ Describe wines with clarity.

- ✓ Recognize major grape varieties and regions.

- ✓ Read wine labels with confidence.

- ✓ Taste wine like a pro.

Whether you're choosing a bottle for a business dinner, recommending wine as a hospitality professional, or simply enjoying wine with friends, this knowledge will enhance your experience.

Now go out there, explore, taste, and enjoy wine with confidence!

Cheers! Salud! L'Chaim! Sláinte! Skål!

NEXT STEPS:
PRACTICE MAKES PERFECT

To help refine your tasting skills, use the learning aids in the next section. Practicing these techniques will quickly build your confidence and expand your wine knowledge!

Thank You

Thank you for taking the time to explore Wine Anxiety: From Confused to Confident.

This book was created for anyone who's ever felt unsure about wine—whether you're selecting a bottle at dinner, trying to impress a client, serving guests professionally, or simply wanting to know what all the fuss is about. You don't need to be a sommelier to speak confidently about wine—you just need a little guidance, a few key tools, and the courage to trust your own palate.

My goal in writing this book was to demystify wine and make it approachable for:

- **Hospitality and winery staff** who want to serve with knowledge and poise

- **Professionals and executives** looking to boost their presence and rapport through confident wine conversations

- **Wine enthusiasts** seeking to deepen their understanding and appreciation

- And anyone who's ever felt intimidated by wine culture or "the rules"

I hope you walk away with:

- A strong grasp of essential **wine vocabulary** Recognition of key **grape varieties** and what they mean in your glass

- Familiarity with how **regions and climates** influence flavor

- The ability to assess a wine's **sweetness, acidity, tannins, alcohol, and body**

- A simple yet powerful **four-step tasting method**

- And the freedom to enjoy wine—without pretense, pressure, or anxiety

Whether you're preparing for a business dinner, refining your hospitality service, or simply enjoying a quiet glass at home, my wish is for you to feel confident, curious, and empowered in every wine moment.

Here's to learning, growing, and discovering the wines you truly love.

APPENDIX I:
18 NOBLE GRAPES CHART

Reds

1. Cabernet Sauvignon
2. Grenache
3. Malbec
4. Merlot
5. Nebbiolo
6. Pinot Noir
7. Sangiovese
8. Syrah
9. Tempranillo

Whites

1. Chardonnay
2. Chenin Blanc
3. Gewurztraminer
4. Moscato
5. Pinot Grigio
6. Riesling
7. Sauvignon Blanc
8. Semillon
9. Viognier

APPENDIX II: WHAT'S ON THE LABEL

Old World Method

Producer — Domaine Bouchard Père & Fils

2004 — Vintage

Region — MONTRACHET

APPELLATION MONTRACHET CONTRÔLÉE

GRAND CRU — Variety (Appellation)

BOUCHARD PÈRE & FILS

ABV

Samantha Sommelier | www.samanthasommelier.com

New World Method

Producer — KENDALL-JACKSON

Special designation — VINTNER'S RESERVE

CHARDONNAY — Variety (Appellation)

CALIFORNIA 2017 — Vintage

Samantha Sommelier | www.samanthasommelier.com

APPENDIX III: WINE REGIONS

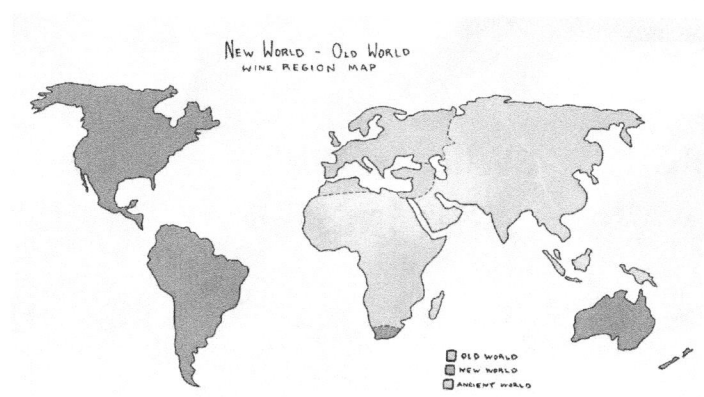

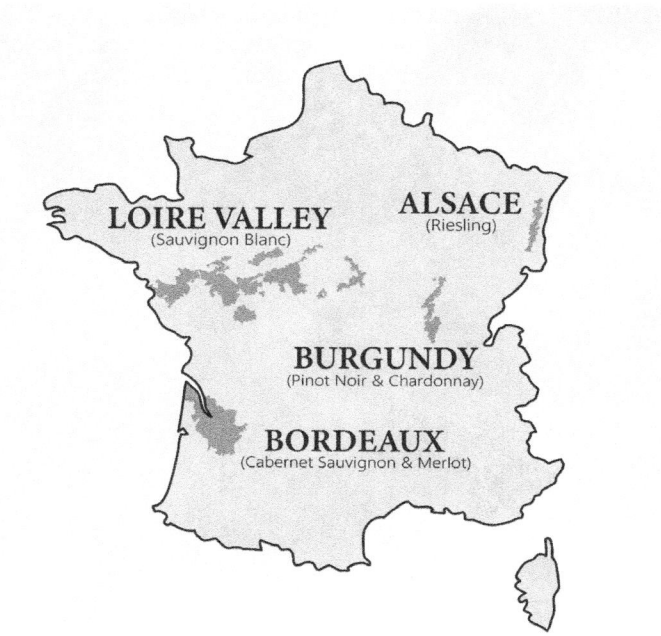

APPENDIX IV: FOUR 'S' SYSTEM OF TASTING WINE

SIGHT	SWIRL	SNIFF	SIP

Look at the color and clarity.	Swirl your glass to release aromas.	Take a short sniff to enjoy aromas.	Sip the wine and savor the taste.

APPENDIX V: REVIEW OF WINE CHARACTERISTICS

Characteristic	Description	Examples	Yacht Insight
Sweetness (Residual Sugar)	Residual sugar left after fermentation. Defines whether a wine is dry, off- dry, or sweet.	Sweet: Sauternes, Moscato, Port Off-dry: Riesling, Gewürztraminer Dry: Chardonnay, Cabernet Sauvignon	First-time drinkers often preferred slightly sweeter wines; experienced guests preferred drier, complex wines.
Acidity	Provides sharpness and crispness; high acidity = zesty, low = soft.	High: Sauvignon Blanc, Champagne Low: Viognier, Malbec	Acidity helped wines stay fresh longer in the cellar.
Tannins	Compounds from grape skins, seeds, stems; create bitterness, structure, and dryness.	High: Cabernet Sauvignon, Nebbiolo Low: Pinot Noir, Gamay	Tannin levels helped guide wine suggestions based on guest preferences.
Alcohol	Affects body, texture, and flavor perception. Higher alcohol = fuller wine.	Low (<12.5%): Riesling, Pinot Grigio Medium (12.5–13.5%): Sangiovese, Chardonnay High (14%+): Zinfandel, Syrah	Lighter wines were chosen for daytime; fuller wines suited elegant dinners.
Body	Refers to weight and mouthfeel. Influenced by alcohol, tannins, sugar, and technique.	Light: Pinot Grigio, Gamay Medium: Sangiovese, Grenache Full: Cabernet Sauvignon, Oaked Chardonnay	Used body comparison (skim/whole/heavy cream) to explain texture to guests.

APPENDIX VI: TOP 10 WORDS TO DESCRIBE WINE

Having a few keywords to describe wine helps improve communication with sommeliers, wine shop staff, and dining companions.

Characteristic	Description
Aroma vs. Bouquet	Aroma = natural grape scent; Bouquet = complex scents from fermentation and aging
Body	Perceived weight and fullness (light, medium, full)
Crisp	High acidity, refreshing sharpness
Dry	Little to no residual sugar—not sweet
Finish	Lingering impression after swallowing; long finish = quality
Flavor Intensity	How strong or weak the wine's flavors appear
Fruity/Fruit Forward	Prominent fruit flavors (not necessarily sweet)
Oaky	Aged in oak barrels; notes of vanilla, toast, spice, or smoke
Soft	Smooth, round mouthfeel with low tannins/acidity
Tannic	Drying sensation from tannins in red wine

APPENDIX VII:
WINE TASTING SHEET

Location & Date – Where and when you tasted the wine.

Grape Variety & Region – The wine's origins.

Appearance – Color, clarity, viscosity.

Aroma – Fruit, floral, spice, oak, earth notes.

Taste & Structure – Sweetness, acidity, tannins, alcohol, body.

Food Pairing Notes – What works well with the wine.

Personal Rating – Would you buy this wine again?

Using a **tasting sheet** is an easy way to **train your palate** and remember what you enjoy.

Location and Date_____

	#1	#2	#3	#4	#5	#6
Winery/Producer						
Vintage						
Color/Clarity						
Aroma						
Body						
Taste						
Finish						

REMARKS

_____

_____

_____

_____

_____

_____

_____

_____

_____

APPENDIX VIII: WINE PRONUNCIATION GUIDE

A beginner-friendly guide to sounding confident when talking wine.

Common Grape Varieties & Styles

Term	Pronunciation
Chardonnay	Shar-doh-nay
Sauvignon Blanc	So-veen-yawn Blahnk
Pinot Noir	Pee-noh Nwah
Merlot	Mer-loh
Cabernet Sauvignon	Cab-er-nay So-veen-yawn
Syrah	See-rah (France) / Shiraz — Shi-razz (Australia)
Riesling	Rees-ling
Gewürztraminer	Guh-voorts-trah-mee-ner
Tempranillo	Temp-rah-nee-yoh
Malbec	Mahl-beck

Sparkling & Fortified Wines

Term	Pronunciation
Champagne	Sham-pain
Prosecco	Proh-sek-oh
Cava	Kah-vah
Port	Port
Sherry	Share-ee

Famous Wine Regions

Term	Pronunciation
Bordeaux (France)	Bor-doh
Burgundy (France)	Bur-guhn-dee
Loire Valley (France)	Lwar Valley
Chablis (France)	Shah-blee
Sancerre (France)	Sahn-sair
Rioja (Spain)	Ree-oh-hah
Chianti (Italy)	Kee-ahn-tee
Barolo (Italy)	Bah-roh-loh
Marlborough (New Zealand)	Marl-bur-oh
Napa Valley (USA)	Nap-uh Valley

APPENDIX IX: WINE TRAITS & FOOD PAIRING BASICS

A simple reference to help you choose the right wine and pairing with confidence.

Wine Trait	Description & Pairing
Sweetness	Check ABV; fruity aromas aren't always sweet.
	Pair with: Spicy foods, desserts, salty cheeses.
Acidity	Zesty, bright, mouthwatering (think citrus).
	Pair with: Salads, goat cheese, seafood, vinaigrette dishes.
Tannin	Dry, puckering mouthfeel.
	Pair with: Red meat, hard cheese, grilled mushrooms.
Alcohol	Adds warmth, body, texture.
	Pair with: Hearty dishes—stews, roasts.
Body	Weight of the wine in the mouth. Match food weight: Light = shrimp, Medium = roast chicken, Full = steak.

Quick Pairing Tips

- What grows together, goes together: Italian wine + pasta, French wine + cheese.

- Balance intensity: Big flavors need bold wines; delicate dishes need lighter wines.

- Sweet balances heat: Choose off-dry wines with spicy food.

- Acid loves acid: High-acid wines pair well with tomato or citrus-based dishes.

- When in doubt? Sparkling wine works with everything!

Made in the USA
Middletown, DE
10 December 2025

22374963R00046